A Thousand Paths to Personal Power

A Thousand Paths to
personal power

Robert Allen

MQP

Contents

Introduction

Some people would like you to think that life is complex and difficult. It isn't. Life is simple and easy. In fact it's so simple and so easy that people can't bring themselves to believe it. Isn't that absurd? They invent complex, convoluted theories to explain what doesn't need explaining and, of course, they pour scorn on what is simple and true. Who ever made money out of simple truth? Who got to be a university professor or a general or a captain of industry by knowing stuff that everyone knows? Nobody, that's who. This book is not full of startling philosophical insights for the good reason that such insights are invariably bogus. The book is full of the sort of stuff that is staring you right in the face and if only you had the common sense to take notice of it your life would improve by several hundred percent. Or you could study a few "ologies," feel clever, and get nowhere.

Creating
your own
Energy

I have a friend who greeted each day by throwing open the window and yelling, "Good morning world!" It got him some funny looks but it seemed to get his day off to a great start.

You never feel so alive and full of purpose as when you are simply very busy.

I have found power where people do not look for it, in simple, gentle, and obliging men without the least desire to domineer…

Friedrich Nietzsche

Life begets life. Energy creates energy. It is by spending oneself that one becomes rich.

Sarah Bernhardt

Physical exertion breeds mental energy and peace of mind. Isn't it annoying that this is what really awful teachers used to tell us at school?

Your well of energy never dries up. The more you dip into it the more you can draw out.

"Life is action, the use of one's powers. As to use them to their height is our joy and duty, so it is the one end that justifies itself."

Oliver Wendell Holmes

You should be open-minded, generous, warm-hearted, and glad. If you are not, then you're doing something wrong.

Into the hands of every individual is given a marvelous power for good or evil—the silent, unconscious, unseen influence of his life. This is simply the constant radiation of what man really is, not what he pretends to be.

William George Jordan

There are many things worth doing with your life but only you can decide what they are.

Don't cling to your achievements, they grow moldy and start to stink. Throw them away and make a fresh batch.

Don't rest on your laurels. When you've succeeded, try something new.

Mental energy isn't like physical energy, the more you use the more you have.

Climb your own personal Everest by all means— but what then?

Think of yourself as a creative person. Decide that your thoughts are of value. However unlikely it seems now it will prove to be a self-fulfilling prophecy.

Some people give out energy like a light bulb illuminates all around it. Others suck it in like a vampire draws blood. You don't need to be that clever to figure out who to associate with and who to avoid.

If you don't meditate, learn. It's easy. It won't interfere with whatever beliefs you hold and it will improve your life by several hundred percent.

Having good ideas is the best way to ensure that you have more good ideas.

The creative spirit lurks
silently deep within us.
You won't find it by
looking but then again
you won't find it by not
looking. The strange
thing is that if you look
hard enough your
creativity will come and
find you.

**Success has ruined
more people
than failure.**

A lighthouse beams its message despite the ferocity of the storm.

Don't bother with all that philosophy and psychology nonsense. Life is tapping insistently at your door and needs to be let in.

How to succeed: try hard enough.
How to fail: try too hard.

Malcolm Forbes

What would you want written on your headstone?

**Highest good is like water.
It benefits creatures without
contending with them and settles
where none would like to live.**

Tao Te Ching

Don't worry about problems. Jumping over hurdles just makes you fitter.

Power is no blessing in itself, except when it is used to protect the innocent.

Jonathan Swift

A bird in flight adapts the power of the wind to its own use.

From little acorns mighty oaks do grow. Imagine you're an acorn, what shape will your tree be?

Learn how to carry your success lightly or it will weigh you down like iron chains.

The vast majority
of creatures
don't even live
long enough to
reach maturity.
We have the
chance to reach
a ripe old age.
What boundless
opportunity!

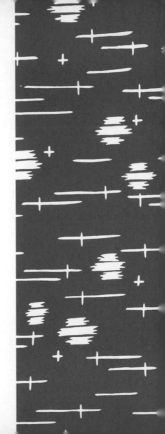

There is a well of energy in your life. As long as you draw from it regularly and wisely, it never dries up.

Get up an hour earlier! No, this isn't a joke—try it. You'll find out what you've been missing, get more done, and enjoy the rest of the day much more.

Problems will make lumps in your thinking if you let them. The lumps become hard to get rid of. Keep your thinking fluid. Let it flow round the problems.

Explore! Life isn't long enough to see even a fraction of what life has to offer, but the more you see, the richer your life will become.

Skill to do comes of doing.

Ralph Waldo Emerson

Every new day is the beginning of the rest of your life.

If you start to take Vienna, take Vienna.

Napoleon

It's hard to admit but what teacher told you about fresh air and exercise was true. A good long walk will invigorate and relax you far better than any pill.

You may be wrong but at least be wrong with a will.

Break the mold. It's easy to get stuck in one way of thinking. Put yourself in someone else's shoes occasionally and get a fresh perspective.

You need enthusiasm. Without it, nothing else works.

Above all, you should foster in children a sense of wonder. That will set them up for life.

Gandhi got his people to stop killing each other not by threats of retribution but by refusing food until they stopped.

Whatever you do you must apply yourself to it wholeheartedly and not give up. After that only the degree of your success remains to be decided.

My mother said, "If you become a soldier you'll end up as a general and if you become a monk you'll end up as the Pope," Instead I became a painter and ended up as Picasso.

Pablo Picasso

Cooking is one of the few forms of creativity that is quick, easy, and provides immense satisfaction both to yourself and your audience.

The most unlikely looking people prove to be a magnet to others simply because of their unbridled enthusiasm.

Go through life singing. It makes the journey more fun.

Old people who have not lost their ability to be enchanted by the world will be happy despite the infirmities of their age.

The beginning is the hardest
part, but determined effort
soon dispels our doubts.

Exuberance is beauty.

William Blake

Vitality!
That's the pursuit of
life, isn't it?
Katharine Hepburn

Luck is great, but to have
the life that makes you
happiest, you have to create
your own good fortune.

Pack as much as you can into life—the time is short and mustn't be wasted.

The main difference between people is not ability but energy.

Moderation, in all things, is good including moderation.

Thinking and planning are great as long as they never get in the way of doing.

I always start a creative writing class by putting **"WRITERS WRITE"** on the board. You'd be amazed how many wanna-be writers entirely overlook this basic fact.

It isn't hard to enjoy life. The trick that some people just don't get the hang of is that there isn't really any trick at all.

Achievement: the death of endeavor, the birth of disgust.
Ambrose Bierce

If you don't have faith in yourself who else is going to?

**Whatever you do, do it with
your sleeves rolled up.**

It's much easier to be happy
and optimistic than miserable
and pessimistic.

**In life, the most valuable word is
"Yes." A life lived in the spirit of
"Yes" will be a full and happy one.**

There is no miraculous change that takes place in a boy that makes him a man. He becomes a man by being a man.

Louis L'Amour

After a failure, you can pick yourself up, dust yourself off, and start again but after a success, you're stuck with it.

Have you ever seen people who walk around like cartoon characters with their own personal storm cloud? There's just no way that they're prepared to let life in and let go of the blues.

Start with a good beginning and it's surprising how the rest falls into place.

The important thing is somehow to begin.
Henry Moore

Walk in the middle of the road and you'll get hit on both sides.

My aunt and uncle wanted a baby
"to complete our happiness."
When the baby arrived it was a little
monster who ruined their lives. If you
don't have happiness right now,
there's nothing that will give it to you.

**Believe that life is good and that
any bad can be made better.
Once you're able to do this,
you're unstoppable.**

There could be no honor in a sure success, but much might be wrested from a sure defeat.

Lawrence of Arabia

If you stop struggling, then you stop life.

Huey Newton

A first rate soup
is better than a
second rate
painting.
Abraham Maslow

**Keep believing in
yourself and you
won't get stuck.
While you think:
"I can do this,"
you can.**

Once you decide to do something
it's surprising how circumstances
conspire to help you.

**Success loves success—failure
loves failure. I'm amazed that
people think there's a choice.**

I once knew a man who, trust me,
had no redeeming characteristics but
one—he had an unquenchable faith
in himself. Amazingly, that alone was
enough to get him through to a ripe
and cantankerous old age.

Okay, it might not work, but if you don't try, how will you ever know?

Don't measure your success in dollars, but in benefit to others.

The successes we haven't yet had look alluring but once we get them they just look tawdry.

I love the part in the movie where the hero says, "I know it's a crazy million-to-one shot but it might just work," and, of course, it does. In life maybe it won't work but we should still have the courage to try.

If everyone achieved all the things they could achieve what a wonderful world we'd have.

Optimism is great, but then you have to put it to good use.

Visualize quite clearly what you want to achieve. Somehow that makes the achieving much easier.

The way to do
is to be.
Tao Te Ching

**Our life is so beautiful and
mysterious that not to investigate
it to the very limits of your ability
is an unspeakable crime.**

Procrastination is a bad habit. The more you put things off, the harder they get.

Put all your eggs in one basket and watch that basket!

Time spent wondering whether you can is wasted. Try and you'll find out soon enough whether you can.

Nothing is impossible. It just hasn't been done yet.

Do without fail what you resolve to do.

In the IT industry they have what they call "deliverables," It means doing the thing you said you'd do, when you said you'd do it at the price you quoted. They regard this as an almost miraculous achievement.

Try not to become a man of success but rather a man of value.

Albert Einstein

The fruit drops from the tree in a split second but how long did it take to ripen?

Stick to your own definition of success and succeed by your own rights.

You've got to be in it to win it.

Victory belongs to he who perseveres longest.

Napoleon

God makes limes. If you want a daiquiri you have to make it yourself.

Nothing is wasted. Our worst disasters teach us priceless lessons.

It is as important to know why something didn't work as why it did.

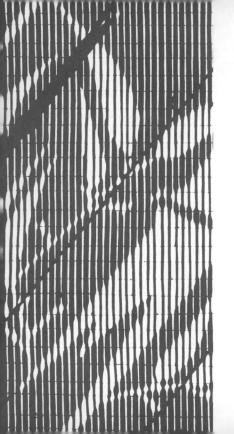

If at first you
don't succeed,
so what?
That's about
par for
the course.

**The reward of
a thing well
done is to
have done it.**
**Ralph Waldo
Emerson**

Live your life as if you will live forever. Don't worry for one moment about dying, because you won't be there when it happens.

Don't mistake activity for achievement.

Think seriously for a few minutes about the consequences of making your first million, and then consider whether you might not spend your time better some other way.

Try to make others as happy as you are, but don't worry about making yourself as rich as others.

Continuous effort—not strength or intelligence—is the key to unlocking our potential.

Sir Winston Churchill

Stick to what you know and do it well, even if there seems to be no market for it. Suddenly you'll find people queuing up to buy.

Work done willingly and well is a form of leisure.

Don't despise the lowly. Where would flowers be without manure?

I spent a lot of time working with very, very clever people. They were, almost without exception, too clever to get anything done or, if they did get it done, it didn't work.

Do the small stuff well but never lose sight of the whole.

Fight the good fight. Most of the time your worst enemy will be yourself. Don't give him an inch!

Work as hard as you can, but not so hard that you're too busy to think, "Is there a better way to do this?"

People want you to be this or that, to think what they think, like what they like and hate what they hate. The hell with them! Please yourself because there is no pleasing the others.

Be the first to take your own good advice.

Don't waste time on quarrels. Most are absurd and take up far more energy than you can afford to invest in them.

The world will always have madmen and wanna-be dictators. It is up to everyone else to make sure there is no vacancy.

I am seeking, I am striving, I am in it with all my heart.
Vincent Van Gogh

One can never consent to creep when one feels an impulse to soar.
Helen Keller

Motivation
and Purpose

In the eating of coarse rice and the drinking of water, the using of one's elbow for a pillow, joy is to be found. Wealth and rank attained through immoral means have as much to do with me as passing clouds.

Confucius

It is desire that drives us to exceed what we believed possible.

Have you noticed how people will do more for nothing than they will if they're being paid. Imagine you're a volunteer.

Without an aim, how can you hit the target?

We grow by solving problems. A quiet life sounds attractive, but think of all the opportunities for growth you'd be missing.

It's said that good intentions pave the road to hell and sometimes that's true. But with bad intentions, it's always true.

Keeping going when you don't think you can is tough, but eventually it pays off and makes you tougher.

What doesn't kill me makes me stronger.
Nietszche

People will do an awful lot just for excitement. If you're lucky they climb mountains or explore trackless wastes, if you're not they start wars.

Once motivated, you can achieve almost anything; unmotivated you can achieve nothing.

A man without a cause has no effect.

Being in want is a great source of motivation. There is nothing that creates inertia so well as satisfaction.

Sometimes you win and sometimes you lose; that's life. What is important is that you never give up trying to win.

You can do whatever you really want to do. The question to ask yourself, therefore, is "What do I most want to do?"

For every man there exists a bait he cannot resist swallowing.

Nietzsche

Some want power, others money, others love, others to save the world. Knowing what motivates people is the key to dealing with them.

Two motives work particularly well—the fear of punishment and the hope of reward.

Before you decide that you have no reason for living, make sure you haven't been living for the wrong reason.

Everyone has a secret ambition. Not to realize that ambition is a tragedy.

Mere curiosity has been the motive for many of the most important achievements of the human race.

Wanting what you've got requires contentment but getting what you want takes ambition.

Necessity is the mother of invention.
English proverb

Love teaches
fools to dance.

Nothing motivates like the forbidden.
A sign that says "KEEP OUT" is
almost an invitation to some people.

To have no set purpose in one's life is the harlotry of the will.

Stephen Mackenna

Desire, fear, and
hope drive us
ever onwards.

"I want to be the world's greatest basketball player," may not do much for you but be sure that it will inspire someone to expend every ounce of his energy.

Power, control, domination; these are the things that keep the world going round and they are not just the province of the mighty. Many ordinary people know the taste and long for more.

What we can't have is alluring, tempting, tantalizing. What is readily available is just boring.

To do the right thing and be praised is good, but to do the right thing even when you get criticized takes guts.

As Mark Twain observed, it's difference of opinion that make horse races. It underpins many other human pursuits too.

Like a traveler with a compass, one who knows what he believes will never lose his way.

It's odd but a hungry, homeless stranger will pick up a foreign language ten times as fast as any pampered school kid.

A strong purpose is a very sharp sword.

Religion is an endless source of inspiration. It has been responsible for some of the greatest deeds of human kindness and cruelty ever seen. It has inspired artists, poets, sculptors, and writers. It is a spring that never dries up, even though the quality of its water varies.

Often the idea of what we want is a far stronger motivator than the possession of the thing itself.

Because it was there.

G. H. L. Mallory's answer when asked why he wanted to climb Mt. Everest

To achieve your aim may take your whole life. In fact, it may even cost you your life. But what would life be without it? Hamlet without the Prince of Denmark, that's what.

To many people, the most inviting phrase in the whole world is, "It's impossible." If flying hadn't been "impossible" we'd still not be able to do it.

Our motives, just like the truth, are rarely pure and never simple.

Discontent is the first step to greatness.

A fire in your belly will help you achieve; a fire in the hearth helps you go to sleep.

Man must work by the sweat of his brow whatever his class, and that should make up the whole meaning and purpose of his life and happiness and contentment.

Chekhov, *The Three Sisters*

It's remarkable how much effort people will expend to get things they don't need.

When I was little I had two teachers. One would start a test by putting a bar of chocolate on the desk to give to the winner. The other placed a leather strap on the desk for the loser. Curiously both methods worked equally well.

Men will do the craziest things just for the love of a woman. And women know it.

Sometimes it is enough just to have the strong desire to do something.

We push all the harder when we have something to push against.

Looking for the money usually reveals the motive.

You'll never find out just what is possible until you've tested the limits and found the impossible.

Strong lives are motivated by dynamic purposes.

Hildebrand Kennet

If your success does not help you grow as a person, does not open your mind to new insights and new aspirations, then it is a poor thing.

What we can gather by way of money and possessions is not of much interest. What we can become as human beings is infinitely more important.

Wanting to do good is a powerful motive. Wanting to do it to others is both powerful and dangerous.

Everyone will tell you, "This is stupid and you should give it up." That's because they can't stand to see anyone with a firmer sense of purpose than their own.

If you must have motivation, think of your pay packet on Friday.

Noel Coward's advice to actors

Interest speaks every language and enables the most unlikely partners to understand each other perfectly.

We learn because it is in our very nature to do so. To grow, thrive, develop, and progress are things that humans do, given even the slimmest of chances.

They say that a bird in the hand is worth two in the bush, but often the prospect of catching those elusive birds is far more alluring than eating the dead fowl.

To accomplish something you need motive, means, and opportunity. Once you have the first then others will soon follow.

Think how many small children have been inspired to achieve the seemingly impossible simply by use of the word "don't."

Ask yourself the secrets of your success. Listen to your answer and practice it.

Richard Bach

Honor and disgrace are things that startle. What does this mean? Honor startles both when it is conferred or when it is taken away.

Keep your own motives clear in your mind. It's easy to lose sight of them in the hurly-burly of activity. If you know why you're doing what you're doing, you are less likely to go wrong.

Virtues and vices are all put in motion by interest.

La Rochefoucauld

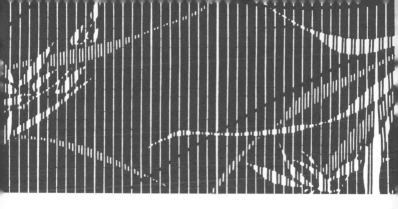

Most people will do a lot for money, but the better ones will do even more for no money.

Love for God has often inspired people to do with enthusiasm all the things God specifically told them not to do.

When I was small, our teacher would throw open the windows and let in the freezing Edinburgh winds. She claimed that no one could learn if they were too comfortable.

Stay curious. Even if you live to be 100 never lose that. It is the thing that will inspire you to get out of bed every morning.

Anyone who knows humans well must have a sneaking suspicion that anything they want to do they will, sooner or later, manage to do.

A powerful motive is like a bolt of lightning. It will cause something dramatic to happen but we can't be quite sure what.

Some rare deer were removed to a nature reserve where they would be safe. They died, one by one. An expert was called in to solve the mystery. He took one look and said, "It's obvious. No wolves."

When I was eight, I stole a candy bar from a shop. I didn't particularly want the candy and I could have bought it but it tasted much, much better for having been stolen.

I happened on the idea of fitting an engine to a bicycle simply because I did not want to ride in crowded trains and buses.

Soichire Honda

Probably every action worth doing had its root in the hope of a parent's praise.

An aim in life is the only thing worth having, and you don't have to be anyone special to have it.

Continuity of purpose is one of the most essential ingredients of happiness in the long run, and for most men this comes chiefly through their work.

Bertrand Russell

What water is to the body, purpose is to the mind.

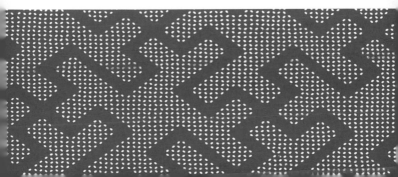

Be careful if you try to motivate people by fear. Once it is let loose, fear can spread like a bush fire and you can never be quite sure who'll get burned.

People will claim the highest motives when performing the basest actions. Keep your eye on the actions.

I want to do it because
I want to do it.

Amelia Earhart

Don't let your
purpose blunt your
humanity.

**Work for something because it is
good, not just because it is easy.**

Desire for fame motivates many people, but it is a road with no end. There can never be enough fame, like there can never be enough money.

If we all simply understood our motives, there would be one heck of a lot of unemployed psychiatrists.

An urgent desire to get ahead is often the direct result of a fear that we may be left behind.

I'm not sending messages with my feet. All I ever wanted was not to come up empty. I did it for the dough, and the old applause.

Fred Astaire

Don't let anyone else tell you what it is in life that you want.

The Scots, largely as a result of their poverty and appalling climate, went out to explore the world. What many would see as disadvantages can be powerful motivators.

People can perform what appears to be identical actions for quite different reasons and that's a great source of confusion. It's important not just to know what people do but why they do it.

You can bet that when the end justifies the means, it'll be a bad end.

Necessity is the mother of taking chances.

Mark Twain

As long as you wish to improve you should never be too happy about who you are.

The stick and the carrot are simple tools. The skill lies in knowing how to use them.

Everything in life must be intentional, and the will constantly taut like a muscle.

André Gide

"Better to rule in hell than serve in heaven," may seem stupid but it explains a lot about people.

A three-foot hole in the ground is just a hole. A six-foot hole is beginning to get personal. By the time a man has dug a twenty-foot hole, it's become *his* hole. He's responsible for the depth, the shape, and the location and he's damned if he'll move it for anyone.

If the creator had a purpose in equipping us with a neck, he surely meant us to stick it out.

Arthur Koestler

It's surprising how many people who have "made it" look unhappier than those who haven't and, what's more, don't care that they haven't.

They say the tower of Babel was a symbol of Man's pride, but it's more likely that once they started building they simply couldn't stop.

People who merely survive from day-to-day seem only half alive. You can see that the humanity has been hacked out of them leaving behind a gaping hole.

Take away a people's sense of purpose and you may as well suffocate them.

In World War I, the troops would sing, "We're here because we're here because we're here because we're here." Sometimes that's all the motivation you need.

Applause is the spur of noble minds and the aim of weak ones.

Charles Caleb Colton

A sense of purpose is like the compass of a ship—you stand little chance of getting anywhere without it.

We are here on earth to do good for others. What the others are here for, I don't know.

W. H. Auden

When you have smashed your enemy into the ground, what precisely have you won?

Millions long for immortality who do not know what to do with themselves on a rainy afternoon.

Susan Ertz

An uncaged tiger is a minor danger compared to a man of purpose.

For many people a purpose is itself, quite enough. The nature of that purpose is largely irrelevant; the fun is in the do-or-die.

We owe the whole of modern science to our own insatiable curiosity. Science may not be much good at answering the question "Why?" but it produces endless amusing and useful answers to the question "How?"

Like all species human beings have one great purpose— to survive. At the moment it is all hands to the pumps.

Progress depends on our unlimited ability to press ahead, not for any well-defined reason, but just because it's what we do best.

The great use of life is to spend it for something that will outlast it.

William James

At one time mere survival was enough motive to keep people going the short distance from cradle to grave. Now the distance is longer and they need as many motives as they can lay their hands on.

It is good to remember that onlookers have a clearer view of the game than the players.

A person with an iron sense of purpose may be wrong, but he'll never be bored.

After many years of trials, tribulations, and effort it may, indeed, turn out that you were wrong. But would you be happier if you never tried at all?

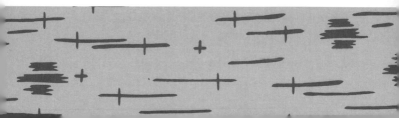

Many people drift through life going nowhere at all. When you see someone with a mission, he stands head and shoulders above the rest.

Learn to bloom where you are planted.

Make it your purpose to find out. Find out what? It doesn't matter— it'll all be useful in the end.

We live with the objective of being happy; our lives are all different, and yet the same.

Anne Frank

Two newlyweds went to see their minister, wearing worried frowns. When he asked what was the matter they said, "We've got no purpose in life."

Success isn't much good in itself. It is the mark of a job well done, but once you have it just stick it in your trophy cabinet and go on to the next job.

Of all creatures, we are the only ones equipped to carry out designs that have nothing to do with our immediate survival. When you've got it, flaunt it.

A man will fight harder for his interests than his rights.

Napoleon

Poverty may inspire people to seek wealth, but wealth inspires its owners to seek more.

We must be the most motivation-conscious people in history. Former generations just did stuff. If they had a motive, they thought it a simple one. We require three months therapy to understand why we take out the trash.

Art for art's sake, with no purpose, for any purpose perverts art. But art achieves a purpose which is not its own.

Benjamin Constant

Many persons have a wrong idea of what constitutes true happiness. It is not attained through self-gratification but through fidelity to a worthy purpose.

Helen Keller

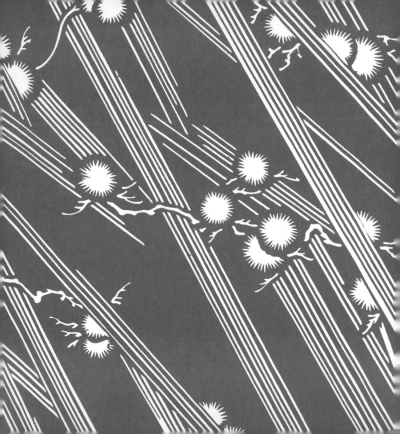

Adapting
to Change

We laugh at the caterpillar
who said of a butterfly,
"You'd never get me up in
one of those things!"
But, who knows, you may
be a caterpillar yourself.

**Since everything must
change, try to make sure
it changes for the better.**

Great things are not done by impulse, but by a series of small things brought together.

Vincent van Gogh

Never regard your self as fully finished. Like a snake you can always split your skin and grow a bit more.

Learn one new thing each day—even if it's only a little one. Over time, you'll be amazed how your mind develops.

A well-travelled German friend told me, "The Americans embrace change for fun, the French for money, and the Germans as an absolute last resort."

We talk of "embracing change" for a reason—it comes as a lover, not as an enemy.

You should change your ideas for the same reason that you change your socks (though not quite so frequently).

When people shake their heads because we are living in a restless age, ask them how they would like to live in a stationary one and do without change.

George Bernard Shaw

Getting older is not really a problem— it's the idea of getting older that causes trouble.

It is only in romances that people undergo a sudden metamorphosis. In real life, even after the most terrible experiences, the main character remains exactly the same.

Isadora Duncan

Be gentle with yourself and others when making changes. Try not to force anything.

Dying is our greatest change and everyone fears it. But ask yourself what a world without death would be like. If there was no Winter, how could you have the Spring?

Handing the world over to the young is the hardest thing to do but also the most essential.

There is nobody who can't change except the dead.

Loving people isn't about changing them to suit you; it's about accepting them as they are.

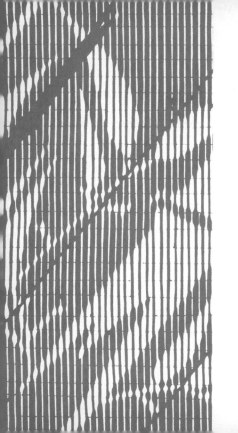

"There is a time for every purpose under Heaven," the Bible says. There is a skill in picking the right time.

Healthy people crave an occasional bit of wildness, a vacation from normality, and a sharpening of appetite. Why, otherwise, did our parents and grandparents tell us that World War II was the happiest time of their lives?

"Everything flows," Heraclitus said. "You can't step into the same river twice." And remember, it isn't only the river that changes.

Some people are proud that their principles are rock-like in their solidity, but few things are right or wrong all the time. Keep your mind flexible or you risk it becoming a fossil.

Good new days are better than the good old days.

As you grow older, you can mature like a fine wine. The alternative is to go off like stale milk.

Remember what that old king had engraved on his ring? "This too shall pass."

Change is the only evidence of life.

Evelyn Waugh

My mother says she didn't mind her 70s but hates her 80s. To my certain knowledge, she said the same about every previous decade. Maybe they're all okay in the end.

"I suppose you've seen a lot of changes in your time," said the reporter to the centenarian. "Yes," replied the old man, "and I intend to see a lot more before I'm done."

My opinion is a view I hold until…well, until I find something that changes it.

Luigi Pirandello

If you work at it, as you grow older, you only change on the outside. Remaining young at heart isn't an accident, it requires effort.

A lot of what changes in life is merely fashion but much of what really matters—love, friendship, integrity— remains the same.

It's strange but true that it is always unhappy people who fear change the most.

People fear change the way they fear the unseen monster in a ghost story. Once you see it, then it's just a guy in a rubber suit.

Always, always have a Plan B.

When he was eight, my son longed to slam-dunk a basketball but, no matter how hard he tried, he couldn't do it. At 17, he can do it with ease. Some changes just take patience.

A rolling stone, they say, gathers no moss. So who needs moss? Rolling can be fun.

Refine your life bit by bit. You don't have to do it all at once, but make improvements day by day.

You cannot change people unless you can give them the desire to change.

Some people choose to finish growing mentally before they hit twenty, others are not finished at ninety. Join the second group, it's more fun.

If you can say, "Wherever I hang my hat is my home," that's a great freedom.

Remember the phoenix and make sure that, when you suffer a fire, you always rise renewed from the ashes.

Keep an open mind and some strange winds may whistle through it, but once you close it, suffocation soon follows.

Life is wiggly like live eels in a bucket. They move constantly because that is the nature of eels.

God, grant me the serenity to accept the things I can't change, the courage to change the things I can and the wisdom to know the difference.

Reinhold Niebuhr

Your home is just a place you live; it's not the shell of a tortoise.
To get too attached to one place is to make a prison for yourself.

In Britain they say, "If you don't like our weather, wait a minute." Life's the same; if you don't like what's happening don't worry, it'll soon change.

If one changes
internally, one
should not continue
to live with the
same objects. They
reflect one's mind
and psyche of
yesterday. I throw
away what has no
dynamic living use.

Anaïs Nin

"It's no good," said our history teacher, "studying Bloody Mary and saying to yourselves 'What a cruel old witch!' Things were different then and if you don't understand that you'll never understand anything."

Change is exciting—like going on a long journey without taking a map.

I have examined myself thoroughly and come to the conclusion that I don't need to change much.

Sigmund Freud

Never look at anything without thinking, "Could that be done better?" The answer is almost certainly, "Yes."

Change doesn't just happen. What you do now affects what becomes of you in the future. Make sure you always look after your future self.

You are a process, not a fixed thing. Even the biggest rock is in the process of crumbling.

Young people sometimes look ahead and say, "I'll never be able to cope with what the future holds." Not so. The person you are now might not be able to, but the person you're becoming will.

You're not a thing, you're a process. Just as an eddy in a stream is constantly changing, so are you. Trying to stay the same is not an option.

We need times when we separate ourselves from family and friends and go to new places. It is only by being without what is familiar that we can be open to change.

People like to do things the same way they've always done them because it saves the trouble of thinking.

If you have enough energy to rip out a vice, you might as well plant a virtue while you're at it.

Change used to be valued for its results, but nowadays it is often seen as a good thing in itself.

Always! That is a dreadful word…
it is a meaningless word, too.

Oscar Wilde

**New things are criticized because
they upset the old order. But it
needs upsetting. A hard shake can
do it nothing but good.**

To change and to improve are
two different things.

German proverb

Like medicine, change can do you good but taste nasty. The pain of resisting change, however, is far worse.

When the British changed currency, people feared the "new money." Now another change is contemplated and people want to cling to the "good old money."

In Scotland I was "that English boy," in England I was "that Scots kid," and in Thailand I was "that foreigner"—and all without changing myself one jot!

There's no growth, no development without change, and the very easiest part is to change your mind. Until you've done that you can achieve nothing.

The thin end of a wedge is a very useful instrument of change.

To never alter your opinion you must be either foolish or dead.

Square pegs, we all know, do not fit into round holes. It is important to know what shape of peg you are.

It's best not to swap horses
when crossing streams.

Abraham Lincoln

However much you change,
you will always still be you
and therefore, in your own
eyes, very much the same.

I look back at my younger self with horror. On the other hand, at least he had enough sense to change into me.

There is a tide in the affairs of men,
Which, taken at the flood, leads on to
    fortune;
Omitted, all the voyage of their life
Is bound in shallows and in miseries.

Shakespeare, *Julius Caesar*

Change yourself rather than your surroundings.

My best friend keeps searching for the perfect job, quite unaware that she will only find it when she becomes the perfect worker.

Fifty-four years
I've hung the sky with stars
Now I burst through—
Crash!
  Death poem of Zen Master Dogen

If you do what you've always done, you'll get what you've always got.

Anonymous

Upon reaching your goal, have a short rest and then set out for the next. Your journey is non-stop.

One day, people will understand the idea that life is change and nothing else.

**All that is not
eternal is eternally
out of date.**

C. S. Lewis

When you run
out of known
paths, the
wild country
is revealed in
its splendor.

My father and I loved to argue so much that sometimes we'd call half-time and change sides. Seeing this, my aunt sniffed disapprovingly and said with some pride that she always stuck to her principles.

Never weep because the world changes. You'd have plenty to weep about if it didn't.

Full fathom five thy father lies;
Of his bones are coral made;
Those are pearls that were his
  eyes:
Nothing of him doth fade,
But doth suffer a sea change
Into something rich and strange.

Shakespeare, *The Tempest*

Progress is about keeping order while things change, yet ensuring change while keeping order.

What sort of doctor does not constantly seek new remedies?

I got to 50 and my friends were talking about retirement, holidays, and a cottage by the sea. Horrified, I started a new career.

The notion that what went before must govern what comes next is cultivated to stop people thinking for themselves.

Not all change has to be useful. You don't repaint the house just to protect the wood, you do it because you want a new color. It is enough that some change is just for fun.

When kids dress in outrageous fashions, their elders don't disapprove because of the clothes but because the kids are saying, "We are the future. We are the people who have come to replace you."

There is not one evildoer who could not be turned to some good.

Rousseau

Changes will come anyway and if you can't be the parent, at least you can be the midwife.

It's always a good idea to let people speak, even if you fiercely disagree with them. Nothing exposes nonsense like a good airing and, who knows, maybe you'll find it wasn't nonsense after all.

Patrick returned to Ireland from America. "The government has changed," his friends told him. "It doesn't matter who they are," he replied, "I'm against them."

Whenever someone says,
"You have no alternative," they are
anxious that you will spot the alternative.

It's traditionally a woman's privilege to change her mind, which just confirms that women are a lot smarter than men.

I went out with a girl who worked in a chocolate factory and, on her first day, they told her she could eat as much of the stuff as she wanted. After a week she hated chocolate with a passion.

If you've done things the same way for a year, it's time for a review. After three years, have a complete rethink and after five years throw everything out and start again.

How many Trotskyists does it take to change a light bulb? "It's not enough to change it, Comrade; you must smash the old one!"

What would be worse—to be told that you will die young or that you will live forever?

Just as we outgrow favorite clothes, we outgrow friends, colleagues, jobs, hobbies— sometimes while they're still in good condition and before we've found replacements.

I wish my mind could drop its dead ideas as the tree does its withered leaves.

André Gide

Your mind is like an attic: it collects junk. Every now and then, you have to look through it and ask, "Do I really need this?" If the answer is "No," then throw it out.

If you want to make enemies try changing something.

Woodrow Wilson

There are two sorts of people best avoided—those who want to change everything and those who want to change nothing.

A new keeper took over the monkey house and gave the animals two bananas in the morning and three in the afternoon. They made a fuss, so he gave them three in the morning and two in the afternoon, and with that they were quite happy.

You have to be on the side of change before you have any right to criticize.

A friend resigned from his job and I asked him why. He said, "Sometimes you just have to leave, even if you don't know where you're going."

Just because something's big does not mean it's invincible. Mountains may appear large and stable, but they are nothing but sand in the making.

We decided to redecorate. Gran said, "But it was a lovely house when you bought it; why do you want to change it?" Maybe because we've lived here ten years.

"If I had my time again, I wouldn't change a thing," said the old man. Wow, what a waste of opportunities!

The more things change the more they remain the same.

Alphonse Karr

There is no shame admitting you were wrong. It merely means you are wiser today than you were yesterday which is, after all, much better than the other way round.

The death of dogma is the birth of reality.

Immanuel Kant

Having one point of view is like keeping your ship in port. What is the point of owning a ship if it never sets sail?

Life flows like a great river. It has eddies, currents, waterfalls, and a thousand surprising twists and turns. To keep up with it, you need a fluid mind.

Life is more like surfing—you need to be lively, responsive, and ready to change at a moment's notice.

If at first you don't succeed, try again. If you still don't succeed, give up and try something else. There are no prizes for lack of imagination.

These days change is so fast and furious that it looks more like a toboggan run. But remember when you were a child just how much you enjoyed sliding.

It's people who are the most uncertain in their hearts who are the most dogmatic in their minds.

"How did you get your husband to agree to change all the furniture?" a woman's friend asked her. "I didn't, I just got him to persuade me what a good idea it would be."

Some things cannot be changed, and then it is wise to consider whether they are worth the trouble of keeping.

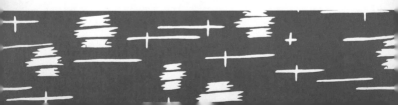

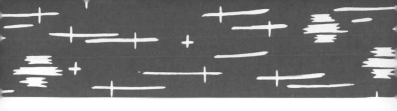

A foolish consistency is the hobgoblin of little minds.

Ralph Waldo Emerson

There's a time for some changes. Why you can give up smoking or go on a diet successfully one day and not on others is a mystery. Knowing how to pick the right moment is an art worth cultivating.

My grandfather would set his wife's newspaper alight while she was reading it. My dad told him it was a stupid, dangerous thing to do, to which he replied, "Aye, but at my age you can do wi' a bit of variety."

Every day, in every way,
I am getting better and better.

Emile Coué

(to be repeated 15-20 times morning and evening)

Communication

A woman left a three-page note for her friend. At the end, she put, "Sorry this is such a long note. I didn't have time to write a short one."

To be simple is the best thing in the world.

G. K. Chesterton

Politeness is an inexpensive way of creating good relations.

They say a lie can be half way around the world before the truth gets its boots on. But squash the lie anyway, because it's important that someone tells the truth, and eventually people may listen.

Everything should be made as simple as possible ... but not simpler.
Albert Einstein

When you meet someone new most of what you have to say to each other is unspoken and happens in those first few vital minutes. This brief period can make or mar a relationship.

Giving people your full attention when they speak is the sincere person's answer to flattery.

Language can be used to enlighten or confuse. Make sure you use words to enlighten and leave the confusion to lawyers.

Helen Keller, though blind, deaf, and dumb, spoke to the whole world.

Music finds its way where the rays of the sun cannot penetrate.

Søren Kierkegaard

Talk to people in a way they'll understand. Jesus talked about sheep and fishermen, not about how many angels could dance on the head of a pin.

Sharing is one of life's major pleasures. The main way to share yourself is to talk to others.

There are men who would quickly love each other if once they were to speak to each other; for when they spoke they would discover that their souls…had only been separated by phantoms and diabolical delusions.

Ernest Hello, *Life, Science and Art*

It's worth considering the effect that your words may have on others. Try them out on yourself first. What sounds okay when it's inside your head can sound all wrong when you say it.

How much time we can waste in carefully composing what we mean to say! In some countries they have a "yes" that means "no" (politely). Being direct without being rude is a useful skill.

The best communication is intended to inform the recipient, not make the writer look clever.

"Say what you mean and mean what you say" may be old advice, but that doesn't stop it being true.

If you can't express what you want to say simply keep thinking about it until you can.

Say something simply, well, and once. The more you elaborate and explain the less people will understand.

Nowadays you can talk to almost anyone almost anywhere at almost any time. The novelty is so great that some people forget you still need to have something worth saying.

Language is one of the greatest human attributes. It is a great responsibility to use it wisely.

Janice, a colleague, always made me feel faintly uneasy. Then I realized what it was. She never said anything at all about herself—none of those little tidbits people share to show they like and trust each other. You don't even notice them until they're missing.

A successful relationship involves constant and plentiful communication.

Simplicity and naturalness are the truest marks of distinction.
W. Somerset Maugham

Talking to teenagers, especially your own, can be troublesome but, no matter how much effort and frustration it costs, it's infinitely better than not talking to them.

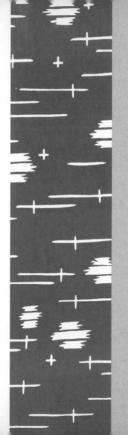

We seek the whole world over and find only what was within us at the start.

Extraordinary how potent cheap music is.

Noel Coward

You have to look beyond language. Americans, British, Australians, and Canadians speak the same language—yet their words mean different things! Effective communication means ignoring the surface of the water and peering at the fish swimming beneath.

A clever idea isn't clever because it's hard for others to understand; it's clever because of its simplicity and that no one else noticed before.

No matter what you're told, always ask: Who? What? When? Where? Why? How? It's amazing how these questions act like floodlights and penetrate the darkest corners.

If you are simple and straightforward and have no secret plan, be sure that people will speak of your great cunning.

Nobody sees what is blindingly obvious until someone else has found a way to express it simply.

Simplicity of expression is like white light, it may look simple but it is actually complex.

What people say is important, but it is much more informative to observe what they do.

People who know each other well—long-time couples, for example—develop a faculty of communication that is largely independent of words. They have felt things together for so long that words have become superfluous.

It's important always to tell the truth to yourself even if, just occasionally, you have to lie to others.

Listen carefully when people speak. However much information they may intend to hide, they will tell you all about themselves if you pay close attention.

A sense of humor is the oil in the communications machine.

I like people who refuse to speak
until they are ready to speak.

Lillian Hellman

No one wants your advice unless
they're paying for it. If they ask for
it, beware. If they don't ask for it,
keep your big mouth shut.

The Romans said that there's truth in wine. This is often a good way to get close to someone so long as you can control the input of wine and the outpouring of truth.

Speech is conveniently located midway between thought and action, where it often substitutes for both.

John Andrew Holmes

I gave a lecture in London and was met with polite silence. I gave the same lecture to an American audience and was met with appreciative murmurs of "Yeah!" "Right!" Good listening is an art.

A complicated idea is often just a lot of simple ones jumbled together. It helps to pull them apart before you get bogged down.

Good communication is like dancing—it's important to be in step with those you want your words to reach.

Remember your alphabetical order—thinking comes before speaking.

A reputation for honesty and candor will stay with you forever. So will the opposite sort of reputation.

Conversation isn't just useful; it's one of life's great pleasures—without it, your inner life withers. Being too busy to chat is almost as bad as being too busy to breathe.

Music is another lady that talks charmingly and says nothing.

Austin O'Malley

There is a saying that beautiful words are not true and true words are not beautiful. Don't you get the feeling that someone said that just because it sounded good?

Being certain you are right makes communication difficult. Entertain the possibility that you may be wrong and you can have a discussion instead of an argument.

Imagine that everything you said has been written down somewhere just waiting to be read back to you. Wouldn't you be more careful how you speak? Just think of all the things you have said that are now stored in other people's memories.

E-mail is such a great tool. Think of the people you'd never write to (too much trouble) or phone (too expensive) but who you can contact by e-mail in minutes, even if they live on the other side of the world.

Some acquaintances of ours make a point of eating in silence. What a waste! Meals are for talking, laughing, discussing, and gossiping.

Communication in every form is so much a part of man as man in the very depth of his being that it must always remain possible and one can never know how far it will go.

Karl Jaspers,
The Perennial Scope of Philosophy

Is it true, as some would have it, that we chatter to avoid "real" communication? I think that the chatter is more to do with real communication than any amount of sober discussion of "issues."

Chitchat is a vital part of communication. It's not what you say that's important, it's the way you say it and all those subtle messages that you convey under the words.

Usually volume is in inverse proportion to content or, to put it another way, if you're right, you don't need to shout.

Quiet, relentless persistence is most effective in an argument.

If you think about what you want to say and cut out all the words you don't need, you can be sure that people will listen to you.

If you find the sound of your own voice attractive, you can be sure that others don't.

As a schoolboy, I once recommended a book to a friend. Thirty years later, a man approached me in a library and introduced himself as that friend. He still read that book regularly and loved it. It's amazing what influence our slightest words can have.

Try to say at least one thing really worthwhile each day.

They used to tell girls that one way of knowing you are in love is when you are more interested in what the other person has to say than in speaking yourself.

Speaking to people who are different from you is one way of looking at yourself in the mirror.

Getting the power to make peace is a difficult, painstaking, time-consuming, patience-trying matter. Any damn fool can make war.

"Everybody's talking at me," the song goes. When the world is so full of information it makes your head spin. You must learn to pick and choose.

A therapist I know told me this: "It's useless telling people anything they aren't ready to understand."

If you are a living example of your beliefs you'll convince a lot more people than if you are simply a propagandist.

When someone annoys you, write them the really hurt, angry, self-righteous letter you'd like to send. Then wait a while, throw it in the trash, and write a proper reply.

Even the most mundane words always benefit from being mulled over for a while. A quick answer is usually one you'll regret.

My friend Paul used to see an old lady each day on his way to the shops. He'd say hello, how are you, nice day—just routine stuff. After she died, she had left behind a letter thanking him for their little chats. They were, apparently, the only ones she'd had.

I've nothing to say and I'm saying it and that's poetry.

John Cage

A conversation in which you are not eager to hear what the other person says is just a lecture.

People who speak rarely are usually worth listening to. Others can speak all day and say nothing much.

You communicate all the time, like it or not. I crossed a road in Israel and a Palestinian taxi driver called, "Hey, you, English!" I asked him how he knew I was English as I'm rather dark for a British person. "Easy," he replied, "you looked the wrong way when you crossed the road."

A smile given to someone who isn't expecting it can be far more welcome than any number of words.

The Greeks used to say that there's no news so bad that an Athenian doesn't want to be the first with it. Isn't it amazing how these Athenians get around?

If you can make people laugh, is that not a wonderful power?

When someone is being difficult always try to keep your patience and smile. That way you leave them room to eventually be less difficult.

To be simple, natural, and unaffected is not something most of us do simply or naturally. It takes practice.

Speak plainly, by all means. Everyone benefits from honesty, so long as it's not used as a license to be rude.

Taking yourself too seriously is a sure way of making others treat you lightly.

People are compulsive communicators but unless we're careful the whole world buzzes constantly with chatter and the message is lost in the noise.

Between what you want to express and what you are able to express, there is always a gap. It may be a small gap or a mighty chasm, but there is no getting rid of it completely.

Speech is the Mother, not the handmaid of Thought.

Karl Kraus

Friendship will not stand the strain of very much good advice for very long.

Robert Lynd

Our forebears, having more time on their hands, took great pains to write long and sometimes tedious books. If you want to keep people interested, you need to go from A to B via the highway and not the scenic route.

It's the things that are hardest to say that are the most important. Deep emotions make us tongue-tied but, even so, these are the times when it's important to say something sincere, even if it's not very clever.

Let your skill with words project your passion. Deep feelings, however genuine, get lost if your manner of expressing them is poor.

It's very good to speak from the heart so long as you check it with your head before you let your words anywhere near your mouth.

Language comes naturally to most of us, but to make it shine you need to polish it a bit.

Some silences speak louder than words. You can learn to express love, anger, and even humor with a well-timed silence.

It's fine to be a person of few words so long as you aren't also a person of few thoughts.

Poetry too readily understood is commonly dispensed with altogether, like conversation after marriage.

Frank Moore Colby

I spend so much time writing books in my head that my family accuse me of not listening to them. "Could you just finish breakfast with us before going back to your readers," they shout.

There is no pleasure to me without communication; there is not so much as a sprightly thought comes into my mind but I grieve I have no one to tell it to.

Montaigne

Make sure you say all the things that need to be said so that, one day, you don't have to think, "I never told X that."

I was once introduced to Geraldine as a psychologist. During the whole meeting, although I said little, she was clearly nervous. Later, when we knew each other better she confided that throughout the meeting she'd been unable to see any further than that one word.

When dealing with people, you need two extra senses: a sense of humor and a sense of proportion.

Read over your compositions, and wherever you find a passage which you think is particularly fine, strike it out.

Samuel Johnson

Accept that you may be wrong and others will accept that they may be wrong too.

There are always words to repair the damage—it's finding them that's the tricky part.

Simplicity, clarity, singleness; these are the attributes that give our lives power and vividness and joy.

Richard Halloway

The more you don't speak to people, the harder it becomes. The silence will turn to hostility even though nothing has happened between you. Break down that wall before it grows too high.

Keeping your feelings bottled up used to be thought good. Why? What good are feelings unless they're expressed?

Have you noticed that when someone says, "You really need to hear this," you usually don't?

Some people have great powers of persuasion. This does not make them right.

Grandmother used to say, "If you can't say something nice, say nothing at all." Of course no one takes much notice but, just maybe, Granny had a point.

To speak to people well, you have to know how they feel inside. You have to recognize the humanity you both share. Otherwise, you may as well read a shopping list.

Can you talk to a whole group of people and make each of them think that you're talking to him or her personally? It's not easy, but it's true communication.

It's good to be close to your friends and tell them everything. That cements the bonds of friendship. But remember that, when friendship ends, everything you've said is now in enemy hands.

Simplicity is the ultimate sophistication.

Leonardo da Vinci

**Look back on what you've said
in the past. If it doesn't make
you squirm, then worry about
how much you've grown.**

Being in the right does not depend
on having a loud voice.

Chinese proverb

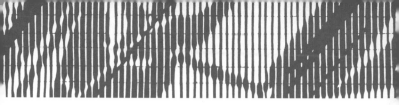

Travel only broadens the mind if you embrace new cultures. If you think only of Pensacola or Birmingham wherever you are, then you might as well stay at home.

I used to work in publishing. Authors would pester the Managing Director for a decision on their books. Little did they know that his Number 1 rule was: "The quick answer is always 'No.'"

Get up and tell them what you're about to tell them, then tell them, tell them what you've just told them and sit down.

Anonymous

When I was a child people used to say, "Fair words butter no parsnips." I always liked that saying, even though I hated parsnips.

The best introduction is, "Hi," said with genuine warmth. It's worth any number of smart remarks.

Be open to people who are unlike you. Their differences can benefit you.

Think what you want to say before you say it. A journey can be the better for having a road map.

These days you have to tell so many people so many things that, unless you make a real effort, you can end up not really communicating with anyone.

The Chinese used to say that one picture was worth a thousand words. What's more, nowadays you can send the picture by e-mail!

Dealing with others requires many qualities, but a sense of humor is indispensable.

A true friend listens sympathetically to your problems and never ever offers any solutions except those you have already found for yourself.

Resist the temptation to tell disagreeable truths—even if it does make you feel better.

Sing in the shower! Make a joyful noise! You may have a truly awful voice, but the joy will still be shared.

If I go to Bermuda and tell you about it when I get back, no matter how eloquent I am, you'll still not have been to Bermuda.

A perfect poem is impossible. Once it has been written the world would end.

Robert Graves

Have you ever noticed how two foreigners forced to communicate in a third language usually do better than native speakers? Communication is not a matter of grammar or vocabulary but of shared feeling and experience.

When you did something good at school, what part was best? Telling your buddies and then your parents.

I know what things are good: friendship and work and conversation.

Rupert Brooke

Why do they call middle class people "the chattering classes?" Don't they think that anyone else can do it?

The Press has an odd way of communicating with their readers...reconfirming to them what they already think.

Who can walk by the sea and throw pebbles into the waves without feeling happy?

You don't have to be good
with words to be eloquent,
but you do have to be good
with feelings.

If you say something really sharp and get a laugh or a round of applause don't be tempted to repeat it.

A good talker is a companion but a good listener is gold.

With those close to you it is important to appear to be completely frank, but more important never to really be so.

Genius is the ability
to reduce the
complicated to
the simple.
C. W. Ceram

Relationships

There is no hope or joy except in human relationships.

Antoine de Saint-Exupery

Know the value of others and acknowledge it. It is a mistake to see others merely as rivals to be defeated.

Always work to create harmony around you. Only fools contrive to unite everyone against them.

In my town there was a notorious junction presided over by traffic lights. One day the lights failed and people had to decide between them whose turn it was. It worked so well that they got rid of the lights.

When angry, bite back the first thing you want to say. Ninety-nine times out of a hundred it'll be better left unsaid.

In certain Buddhist monasteries they say, 'If not me, then who?' It means just do the chores and don't stop to argue about whose turn it is or whether it's fair.

He does good to himself who does good to his friend.

Erasmus

The art of good relationships is never complete— you have to keep working at it.

Never assume that your colleague is dull—you could be the one who's dull.

A horse can pull a cart that a man could not move one inch. The man tells the horse to go, stop, turn left, turn right. So why do they call it horsepower?

Be nice to people on your way up. You may meet them again on the way down.

You can do without family but you need someone you can trust. If all else fails, buy a dog.

Humans have their faults, but they are the only creatures that have the urge to protect the young of others and even of other species.

The purpose of the human race is not winning.

Man's best support is a very dear friend.
Cicero

Eat together—not just at Thanksgiving and Christmas but all the time. Nothing cements a family like a good meal.

Wear a smile and have friends; wear a scowl and have wrinkles.

George Eliot

If you want a family to function well, you have to share each other's interests. My son tells me stuff about football. I hate football but I'm glad that he tells me.

A fly may walk with impunity on the lip of a lion.

I've friends I've had for 30 years and although we don't see each other often, when we do meet, the time between counts for nothing.

Never ever give up on anyone. The most unlikely people will come round in the end if they feel that somebody is there for them.

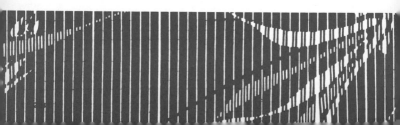

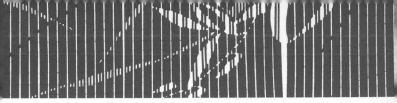

It is said that all happy families resemble each other, but that unhappy families are unhappy in their own way.

No one in their right mind could say why they want children but, even so, they feel their absence.

From time to time ask yourself, are people any better off for knowing you?

Work is one of the few places (outside prison) where you can spend all day cooped up with people you don't choose to know. Humor and tolerance are essential.

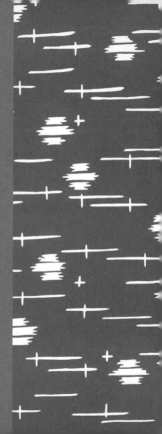

If bees, ants, and other creatures can work together harmoniously, surely people can learn to do the same.

Our families force us to accept some people, warts and all. It's hard to do, but it is good preparation for life.

A companion is good to have, but one who tells you the truth is better.

A Thai friend taught me that when friends let you down, you should not reject them but put them to one side for a little while to see if they improve. I've tried this and it works.

Remember to forget— don't just forgive.

Why is it too much trouble to cook for yourself? Because cooking is more about sharing than it is about food.

Even the least gifted of us can cultivate the art of friendship.

The only way to have a friend is to be one.

Ralph Waldo Emerson

There is no end of books teaching you how to be a spouse or a parent, but no one needs a book to teach them how to be a friend.

Good company and good discourse are the very sinews of virtue.

Izaak Walton

It is no wonder that someone founded a financial empire on the simple idea of helping people find their old school friends. What an irresistible bargain!

A family isn't an army led by a general (male or female!); it's a community.

There are people you know you want to be close to just by looking at them and others you don't like until you've had a damn good quarrel.

A good relationship can develop after you no longer count what it costs you.

Friendship is the only cement that will ever hold the world together.

Woodrow Wilson

Those who say that a platonic friend is merely one they haven't slept with yet simply reveal their own inadequacy in both departments.

Friends, family, and a quiet mind are your true wealth.

If someone knows all about you and still loves you, that person is a true friend.

Those closest to us are the safety net that waits for us whenever we fall.

Do not remove the mosquito from your friend's brow with a hatchet.

Chinese proverb

Between writing the last path and the next I e-mailed a friend in Australia and got a reply. Nothing has done so much for friendship as e-mail.

People will judge you by your companions as much as your actions.

A friend is a powerful person; the guardian of your secrets. Just remember that before it is too late.

Ask yourself whether you would do for others everything that they would do for you.

It's more difficult to be patient than angry—for everyone (not just you).

We all have an unending ability to take others for granted. Why?

It's the friends you can call up
at 4am that matter.

Marlene Dietrich

**La Rochefoucauld called friendship
"only a reciprocal conciliation of
interests," which leaves the rest of
us feeling sorry for the poor sap.**

The bird, a nest; the spider,
a web; man, friendship.

William Blake

Your belief in people brings them to full bloom.

Do not judge others (or yourself) on failure—failure is seldom fatal.

God gave us our friends to make up for our relations.

If you can't give, you won't receive.

Never be too busy for someone, even when you really are.

Have faith in others
and they will have
faith in you.

**Visit those you like often,
but stay briefly.**

When someone finds it necessary to say, "Trust me"—don't.

A mark of a good relationship is the sheer number of things you don't have to say.

When you meet a really good friend, it is like finding your long-lost sibling.

They say that a friend in need is a friend indeed. But what about a needy friend?

It's those who stick around when the road gets rough that are the friends worth keeping.

Animals are a lot less frustrating than people. They don't offer advice, don't ask for any, and never attempt to borrow money.

Good company makes a feast.

Learn to listen to the problems of others, learn to accept their success.

If you don't have people you are close to, then everything else you have doesn't count.

Stress relief beyond belief is a smile.

Material wealth is pointless if there's nobody to share your happiness with.

Friendship is the pleasing
game of interchanging praise.

Oliver Wendell Holmes

**True companionship brings on a
feeling quite like having completed
a good meal.**

Compared to everyday relations with the world, love is easy.

Caring about others makes the most trivial and inconsequential things become a source of great satisfaction.

Liking the same things is fun, but disliking the same things can be intoxicating.

A friend is like a poem.

Persian proverb

It's worth thinking about this from time to time: if you got run over by a bus, how many people would miss you, and how much?

Go oft to the house of thy friend, for weeds choke the unused path.
Ralph Waldo Emerson

A kindness done is good for everyone.

Those who seek an advantage are not worth your trust.

Always think of others as your equals—that way, they might just reciprocate!

Share your joy with others, not your suffering.

A good marriage is your castle, but a bad one is your prison.

A broad smile and a big "hello" brightens everyone's day.

You have to like yourself. It seems obvious but many people fail to do it.

Friendship is love without his wings!
Lord Byron

People who develop special tactics for "getting away from the family" are missing something.

If you're too important to have time for others, then you're not as important as you think.

A true companion is a gift from you to you.

Have no companions not equal to yourself.
Confucius

"My friend's friend is my friend," may be true in politics but for everyone else it's nonsense.

If you would be wise you should befriend the wise.

Cultivate in yourself the qualities you admire most in others.

He does good to himself who does good to others.

If you do not know somebody wise enough to accompany you it is better to walk alone.

Cultivate relationships with those who are good-hearted and level-headed.

Always try to be a light in other people's lives.

When you love people, is it for your benefit or theirs?

Like wine, good buddies improve with age.

Two friends—two bodies with one soul inspired.

Homer

No one is so rich that he can afford to throw away friends.

Of my friends I am the only one left.

Terence

In choosing friends, quality rather than quantity is important.

Avoid those who delight in misery and seek those who laugh a lot.

Be slow in choosing a friend, slower changing.

Benjamin Franklin

You may not always have happiness, but you can always be the cause of it in those around you.

People will know you by your actions toward others.

Have plenty of young companions—it makes reading the obituary columns less melancholy.

My young friends keep me jolly and my old ones keep me warm.

Character

Life is not
worth living
until you
have made
it that way.

The
greatest
battle in
life is to
overcome
yourself.

Fears are bullies and cowards that sneak around in the dark corners of your mind. Drag them kicking and screaming into the light and they run away.

You may think your life is small and ordinary, but everyone has the power to do good.

When someone makes you angry, imagine a friend had done it. You'd forgive the friend, wouldn't you?

If there is no wind—row.

Latin proverb

A smile packs more power than a frown and uses less energy.

You know when a child goes on and on and on and on? Persistence works.

There is no evil in the atom, only in men's souls.

Adlai Stevenson

Remember the lone student who faced a tank in Tiananmen Square? It is the courage of the student, not the power of the tank, that we remember.

Should you associate with people of poor character? If you stood on a chair holding a rope and someone was below holding the other end, which would find it easier to pull the other to him? Suppose the person below was drowning?

Women and judo players know that appearing to be the weaker contestant is the way to win.

If you want to gamble in life, you should bet on yourself.

Your beautiful thoughts may be interesting, but people value you for your beautiful deeds.

What we think, we become.

Buddha

Wisdom is worth more than wealth, looks better on you than smart clothes, and keeps you warmer than the finest house.

The world pretends to admire the wise but appreciates the foolish. However the pursuit of wisdom is worth far more than the admiration of fools.

Dignity does not consist in possessing honors, but in deserving them.

Aristotle

Live your life as though you were drinking fine wine. Savor every mouthful right down to the very last drop.

However much you try to hide it, people know what you're really like. The only thing to do is to improve.

Once you choose to let it, life will flow through you like a great surge of electricity. All you have to do is turn on the switch.

Don't rely on others, but make sure that others can rely on you.

Have you ever noticed how people of exceptional character enrich our lives just by being who they are?

Laughter lifts the spirits, deflates pomposity, and mocks bigotry. Plus it's free!

Conserve your energy—life is not a renewable resource and it makes no sense to fritter it away on trivial problems.

There is nothing in which people more betray their character than in what they laugh at.

Goethe

Always do right—this will gratify some and astonish the rest.

Mark Twain

Believing other people's publicity merely makes you gullible, but to believe your own is fatal.

Only one idea in ten actually works. To succeed, you need to drip ideas like a leaky faucet.

Imagine you could do anything you wanted, only every time you did something wrong, a person in China would die. Would the Chinese be safe in your hands?

The only way to defeat an idea is to have a better idea. Bombs and bullets can't hit ideas.

If you need a helping hand, you've got two—one at the end of each arm.

Don't spend time worrying about the future when you could be helping to make the future.

Don't worry about nurture versus nature. Just grab your life in both hands and make of it whatever you can.

If you want a thing done, go; if not, send.

Benjamin Franklin

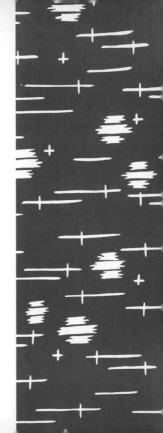

The only resource that will never dry up on you is yourself.

When you want to make a difference and benefit the world, it's best to start with yourself.

Heaven and hell are both real. They lie within you and can be summoned in a second but, once summoned, they are not so easily dismissed.

People aren't horses and you can't train them with the bridle and the whip. The only way to deal with them is to learn to love them.

No one ever got better who did not want to get better. The wanting is the start of everything.

Making yourself into something means carving the wood of your own existence. That may be painful but think of the finished article!

Circumstances do not make a person but they show that person for what he is.

Other people's experience can be interesting, but only your own can change you.

Neither fire nor wind, birth nor death can erase our good deeds.

Buddha

Character comes from hard work and constantly surmounting problems. There is no easy path.

The Chinese say that a man who stands straight need not fear a crooked shadow.

Men of genius are admired, men of wealth are envied, men of power are feared; but only men of character are trusted.

Alfred Adler

Like reading, chess, or playing the fiddle, happiness is just something you learn.

**Do the very best you can
with the sense you've got.**

A fool who knows
he is a fool is not
a great fool.

**Character, true character, is as
hard and enduring as diamonds.**

I read about the young yachtswoman Ellen MacArthur climbing her mast in a storm to make a vital repair. I've never sailed. The very thought makes me sick. But now I know that should the eventuality arise, I too would feel compelled to climb the mast.

You can fool everyone else for a while, but you can't fool yourself. Mess around and sure as anything the person in the mirror is going to get you.

Character is a diamond that scratches every other stone.

Don't drop your ideals just because the world will not embrace them. The world and you would be a lot worse off without them.

If you always try to do right, people may not notice, but if you once do wrong, they'll never let you forget.

Virtue is not virtue if it is merely the result of insufficient temptation. To be real virtue it must be the very fiber of your being.

People think the devil within them is strong, but in truth he's weak, silly, and ignorant. If he weren't, how did he get to be a devil in the first place?

Let what you do speak louder than what you say.

Don't blame others for your misfortunes—you can't change them but you can change yourself.

The first step to happiness is to lay claim to your own life, warts and all.

**Champions take responsibility.
When the ball is coming over the
net you can be sure I want the ball.**
Billie Jean King

Good character is not a
monopoly of the clever or the
successful; it belongs to
anyone who has the strength
and determination to foster it.

**God may give you nuts, but he
expects you to crack them yourself.**

A true knowledge of ourselves is a knowledge of our power.

Mark Rutherford

"I am the master of my fate; I am the captain of my soul" may not be completely true, but you should act as though it is.

Anyone can triumph over past and future problems, but it takes character to triumph over today's problems.

Simple virtues are despised only by those incapable of having them.

Life isn't hard; it's people who make it hard. It isn't complicated; it's just tricky to see how simple everything really is.

If you find life plain, boring, and unsatisfying it's not life's fault.

Every moment of life is the most exciting, unbelievably miraculous thing you could imagine. Once you appreciate this, then even washing the dishes cannot be despised.

Reputation is what the world thinks a man is; character is what he really is.

Suppose you were made of glass and everyone could see what went on inside your mind. How would you feel then?

If you think you are a fine person and it's all those others who are wrong, maybe you should think again.

The world would be a wonderful place if only we'd shut up and let it.

You can tell what a man is by what he does when he hasn't anything to do.

Only chickens have a wishbone. People have to make do with backbone.

People learn fear as children, but as adults they can unlearn it.

If fear has any use, it is to be a spur to courage.

Judge of your natural character by what you do in your dreams.

Ralph Waldo Emerson

Since we can easily imagine ourselves as being better than we are, would it be so much trouble to make the vision reality?

He who is narrow of vision cannot be big of heart.

Chinese proverb

Do not be embarrassed by joy, even though it seems a little excessive in our troubled times. The Chinese have a proverb that says a single joy scatters a hundred griefs.

You are, at bottom, a much better person than you ever suspected.

Two-thirds of help is knowing how to give courage.

Human beings never cease to be amazed at how brave they are in a crisis.

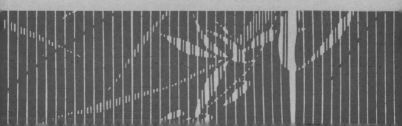

In a crisis don't lean on anyone else; that way you won't be let down. A "No" uttered from deepest conviction is better and greater than a "Yes" uttered merely to please or, what is worse, to avoid trouble.

Real courage is looking life full in the face and then living it to the full.

Whenever you look at an old person, does it occur to you how much courage it took to just get there?

All people have within them the seeds of immense greatness. All you need do is water them regularly.

The world is embarrassed by simplicity and goodness and therefore hides in cleverness and complexity. Fortunately, simplicity and goodness won't go away.

People are fundamentally good, though no one has bothered to tell most of them.

Gandhi

You have a whole store of fine qualities that you have not yet discovered. Put yourself to the test and you'll find them soon enough.

Words have the power to both destroy and heal. When words are both true and kind, they can change our world.

Buddha

The power of vision is uniquely human. It is not what you expected or even what you could have imagined and that is what makes it so great.

You may be satisfied with your circumstances, but only a fool is ever satisfied with his achievements.

If you are driven by the love of money, or fame, or status, then you'll never be satisfied because there is no end to these things.

Only humans are capable of using their intelligence to convince themselves to do what is wrong.

Cleverness that is not harnessed to anything lies with its wheels spinning in the air. Goodness is goodness whatever its position.

"Why do you come to me for enlightenment?" demanded the Zen master. "You have your own treasure house; why don't you use it?"

If we live good lives, the times are also good. As we are, such are the times.

St Augustine

When life gives you lemons, make lemonade.

Study and grow, study and grow! The ability to do this is what makes us truly human.

Be thine own palace,
or the world's thy jail.
John Donne

The more you do, the more
you find you can do. The less
you do, the harder it gets to
do anything.

A man who finds no satisfaction in himself seeks for it in vain elsewhere.

La Rochefoucauld

**It's no good seeking paths.
Paths are made by walking.**

Fulfillment

Living well and beautifully and justly are all one thing.

Socrates

To create something like the Mona Lisa from little blobs of colored oil...now that is real power.

A friend joined one of those "you can do anything if you try hard enough" organizations. Then she found she couldn't become pregnant. Sometimes you must accept limits to your power.

Sometimes all you can do is laugh. If you can laugh, you're not sunk yet.

You needn't achieve great things. Not everyone can change the world. But even modest achievements that take time, trouble, and effort will light up your life.

Every being spends his life searching for that which he hopes will make him happy. Fulfillment lies in finding it.

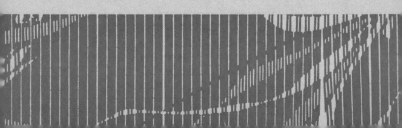

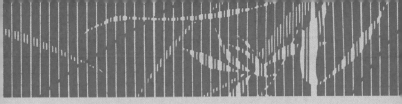

There are few pleasures in life to beat the contemplation of a good job well done.

Making people contented also makes them good, but making them good will not necessarily make them happy.

If your religion or your politics make you and others unhappy, change them.

The joyfulness of a man prolongeth his days.

Psalms

Some people say, "Live hard, love hard, die young." What's so great about being dead? When you're getting the best out of life, you'll want to come back for more.

Live all you can; it's a mistake not to. It doesn't so much matter what you do in particular, so long as you have your life. If you haven't had that, what have you had?

Henry James

We were constructed to survive. Our capacity for happiness is something we've invented for ourselves, and it was one of our better ideas.

If you want to die happy, you must learn to live mightily.

If even the most desperate and impoverished can find time to make music, dance, and have as good a time as their circumstances allow, surely we who are fortunate can do at least that well.

This is life—invigorating as a cold shower and warm as comfortable house shoes. Enjoy!

You reap what you sow in this life. Better make sure you sow joy.

Nothing can bring you peace but yourself.

Ralph Waldo Emerson

Mirth is better than fun, and happiness is better than mirth.

William Blake

The principle business of life is to enjoy it. Anyone who does not know that is wasting his time.

To be truly happy in this life, you need to love others and share with them. Anything less is a poor substitute.

Good friends, good books and a sleepy conscience: this is the ideal life.

Mark Twain

Just as a cat is not the same as a tiger, pleasure and amusement are not the same as happiness, even though they are related.

Nowhere in The Bible does it say that Jesus laughed. That is not, as the sober would have it, because He didn't, but because it is too obvious to be worth mentioning.

Satisfaction is what thinking people have instead of amusement.

Happiness is a matter
of being, not having.

**One way to be comfortable
with one's life is to stop
worrying about the possibility
of being miserable.**

A wise tramp enjoys the world
more than a foolish king.

Manifest plainness
Embrace simplicity
Reduce selfishness
Have few desires.

Tao Te Ching

Why, in a world that gives us so many opportunities, would some people choose not only to be miserable but also to believe that it's doing them good?

There is nothing so conducive to happiness as a sense of achievement.

I was well into middle age before it struck me that there was absolutely nothing to prevent me from being as happy as I wanted.

Learn how to feel joy.
Seneca

Happiness is obvious to those who have it, but utterly mysterious to those who don't.

Whatever you say about happiness sounds like a motto from some tacky souvenir ashtray. This doesn't devalue happiness; it just demonstrates how widely the idea has caught on.

A trouble shared is a trouble halved, but a joy shared is a joy doubled.

The stiff and straight are the comrades of death; the soft and supple are the comrades of life.

Having pleasure yourself is fine but, for it to qualify as happiness, you have to share it with someone else.

It is a fine thing to pursue happiness, but it is much better to create it.

Your life may not be perfect but as long as it's what you want and not what someone else thinks you ought to want, you'll be happy.

"The best things in life are free" is more than a cliché, worse than a truism—it's actually true.

Many people talk about all the things they'll no longer have to do when they retire. Not me. They'll have to drag my cold, dead fingers from the keyboard. No amount of idleness makes up for the loss of work that you love.

The righteous are seldom happy, so they have to make do with being right.

Nothing is more hopeless than a scheme of merriment. Samuel Johnson

It's all a matter of attitude— success tends to go on succeeding and failure sure as heck goes on failing.

Do not worry; eat three square meals a day; say your prayers, be courteous to your creditors, keep your digestion good; exercise, go slow and easy.

Abraham Lincoln

If you can be happy while you wait for a late bus on a rainy morning in December then you've figured it out.

Happiness is like money. When you have a certain amount, it just keeps making more and more.

Joy is the only thing that grows greater the more times you divide it.

A person who consumes happiness usually produces more than he consumes.

The only thing happiness and misery have in common is that those who have them are too willing to share them with others.

Do all the good you can,
By all the means you can,
In all the ways you can,
In all the places you can,
At all the times you can.

Anonymous

When I started to write full time, a friend sent me a drawing to hang over my desk. It shows a heron trying to swallow a frog while the frog is doing his best to strangle the heron. The caption is, "Never ever give up."

Perfect happiness is the absence of striving for happiness.

Chuang-tse

Get off your butt and do something useful. The work is part of the training.

Zen master Hakuin

Happiness is like a fine wine; you don't need much for the flavor to seduce you completely.

Happiness has its foundation in good health.

We all need something to do, someone to love, and something to hope for.

Don't constantly look back on the supposedly golden past, but stride forward to the future, confident that you can make it golden.

If only we'd stop trying to be happy we'd have a pretty good time.

Edith Wharton

When any glassy-eyed zealot promises to make you happy, chase him out of town. Happiness is gentle and eschews fanatics.

It's okay to be miserable sometimes. It's the only way you can know what happiness is.

"Would you rather be right or happy?" is a trick question. If you're happy, you'll be right, although not vice versa.

No one makes us happy or wretched; we decide the matter with our own deeds.

To whomever knocks on your door offering political or religious bliss just say, "No thanks." If they had it they'd know better than to force it on others.

People think they'll be happy when they have nothing to do, but that's just a blueprint for misery. Keeping busy is what happiness is all about.

Seek not happiness too greedily, and be not fearful of unhappiness.

Tao Te Ching

If you really want to be happy, you must learn to feel deeply. Life is an ocean, not a puddle.

People say, "I'd be happy if only I had so-and-so." Not true. If you can't be happy here and now, then you can't be happy at all.

Mark Twain wrote, "To be busy is man's only happiness." As someone who lost his fortune and was predeceased by most of his family, he probably knew what he was talking about.

Always have an open mind—you need plenty of places for happiness to get in.

If you have to stop and consider whether you are happy, you are not.

Sometimes happiness is just like a cat. Go and offer to make friends and it'll run away, but sit down and feign disinterest and nothing will stop it from rubbing up against your legs.

The unexamined life is not worth living.

Socrates

Die when I may, I want it said by those who knew me best that I always plucked a thistle and planted a flower where I thought a flower would grow.

Abraham Lincoln

Don't waste time on anger, or ambition, or envy. These things drive out happiness and bring you nothing but pain in its place.

Life, as John Lennon said, is what happens to us while we're making other plans. He might have added that life has a wicked sense of humor.

Be sure that no politician in the entire history of the world ever made anyone happy.

Some people have a talent for happiness just as some have a talent for music. We can't all be great, but everyone can at least learn to play chopsticks.

The centipede was happy quite
Until a worm in fun
Said, "Pray which leg goes after
which?"
At which he tumbled into a ditch
Considering how to run.

You shouldn't think too much
about happiness.

A good long walk in interesting scenery followed by hot coffee by the fireside...what could be better than that.

Happiness is not a goal in itself—it is a side effect of living your life wisely.

You didn't get here by accident; you planned it every step of the way whether you know it or not.

Quite often you can't tell what happy people are actually happy about; they just feel that way and that's good enough for them.

Warm-hearted, tolerant people are happy. Cold-hearted, narrow-minded people are miserable and make others so.

Give a man health and a course to steer and he'll never stop to trouble about whether he's happy or not.

George Bernard Shaw

Paddling your own canoe is a sure way to find happiness.

Having an aim and pursuing it enthusiastically are essential to happiness. Reaching your aim is just an added bonus.

If you want to be happy as you journey through life, never let go of your sense of humor. It'll help you through the rough patches more than a stout stick will help you up a steep climb.

Money, sex, drugs, and power can all divert us. Unfortunately, they divert away from happiness and not towards it.

Everyone chases happiness, oblivious to the fact that it is chasing them.

Don't pursue happiness; you'll never catch it that way. Get your mind right and you'll find that happiness was there all along.

The Zen master Dogen said; "Do not expect necessarily to be aware of your own enlightenment." He could have said the same of happiness.

Some people seem to think that happiness is contagious and if only they stay close enough to happy people, they'll catch it themselves. Nice theory—but it doesn't work.

People can give you all the good advice in the world, but only you can decide to take it.

Keep busy enough that you leave yourself no time to be unhappy.

Happiness is not a horse you cannot harness it.

Chinese proverb

Look deeply into the nature of things. This is difficult and time-consuming but it brings with it the greatest happiness.

**Circumstances—
what are circumstances?
I make circumstances.**

Napoleon Bonaparte

A man is only ever really
miserable if he thinks he is.

If you are wise but not happy,
then you aren't very wise.

If you want to be
happy, don't
compare yourself
with others.

A great deal of happiness depends
on having good digestion.

Humanity has the power to feed the starving, house the homeless, and heal the sick. Isn't it high time we did it?

If you set out to make others happy, you'll end up making everyone miserable. But you can help them find happiness for themselves— that's a much less meddlesome task.

When I had a regular job, I used to spend hours worrying about what would happen if I lost it. Now I'm a writer—just about the most insecure profession you can think of—and I'm happy.

It is possible to be too clever for your own good. Happiness requires a certain simplicity of spirit.

Only once you accept responsibility for your own life does that life truly belong to you.

When asked to write twenty words about themselves, most people speak about their work.

Happiness comes as a result of helping others.

If you are not naturally contented, then cultivate contentment. There is no end to wanting and no peace of mind if you follow that route.

It's all the little things that make people happy.

The mere sense of living is joy enough.
Emily Dickinson

So many people over many centuries have written about the secrets of happiness that it is amazing there are still so many who don't have it.

In your search for happiness, look after yourself. You weed your garden, have your car serviced, and repaint your house, so why neglect your body?

Above all to thine own self be true.
Shakespeare

If the happiness of others makes you happy, it's likely you are happy by nature.

Life delights in life.
William Blake

How many people
have found that
throwing yourself
into your work
wholeheartedly
increases happiness
and relieves misery?

Happiness is like dancing. The object is to enjoy it from minute to minute, not to race through it to get to the end as soon as possible.

Producing something well is a source of deep satisfaction.

The devil finds work for idle hands.

Be happy and make others around you happy. If you don't do these two things, then the rest of your life is trash.

Some people assume that suffering is character-building. It isn't. Happiness, however, is.

Happiness is not the end of life, but it's an excellent companion on the journey.

Happiness is not a destination—it's a mode of transport.

Choose carefully what you pay attention to and what you ignore, both inside yourself and in the world. These things make up your life.

Following the herd is great if
you happen to be a cow.
People shouldn't live in herds.

Never keep up with the
Joneses. Be happy and let the
Joneses keep up if they can.

Plenty of people are happy
without having the least
idea that they are.

If you always feel you have enough, you'll be happy if you don't; regardless of how much good fortune you enjoy, happiness will elude you.

Be who you would seem.

Greek proverb

Be pleasant to people whenever you can. It sounds simple, is simple, costs little, and contributes both to your happiness and theirs.

Give a flower and the scent
lingers on your fingers.

Chinese proverb

Some people find it hard to be happy
because one day we all die. The fact is
that miserable people die too.

The pursuit of happiness is tiring. Why not just make your own?

Happiness is not the destination—it's the manner in which you travel.

To be happy, you don't need to win battles; you need to avoid fighting them. A skilled general is no match for a skilled peacemaker.

The most miserable person I know was blessed with intelligence, education, and inherited money.

Humanity has developed because some people were brave enough to push beyond the boundaries of what was known.

A man who was being chased by a tiger fell over a cliff but clung on to a vine. Just then, two mice began to gnaw through the vine as he hung in mid-air. He spotted a wild strawberry and, on impulse, put it in his mouth. Delicious!

Zen tale

It is not our position but our disposition that makes us happy.

If your life isn't what you wanted, beat yourself up but nobody else.

The main source of happiness is to be in control of your own life. Not having someone telling you what to do is worth thousands of dollars a year.

Be the new broom that sweeps clean. Your life urgently needs sweeping.

Inner
Strength

Grass breaks concrete. Rust breaks iron. Water wears away rock. It is not the hardest things that survive.

Like a boxer, you have to learn to roll with the punches.

Japanese children are given little Daruma dolls weighted at the bottom so they stand up if knocked over. "Seven times down, eight times up," is a saying they all know.

Do you work to live or live to work, or are you just too busy to ever think about it? Making sure that your motives are clear will help you achieve your aims.

The President of the USA has one type of power but the Pacific Ocean has another. Which would you rather be?

Remember to give yourself time to rest. Treat yourself with consideration and you'll always have energy, but demand too much and you'll start to slow down.

Sometimes effort can seem enough in itself. Just trying hard can be satisfying. But don't get so caught up in pushing that you fail to see where you're going.

Power can only come from within; no one can give it to you.

Strength used
to crush those
around you
will eventually
crumble.

**Use your strength
to benefit others
and it will flourish.**

Termites are tiny, yet they can build huge mounds. Sometimes power comes from cooperation.

You want to be tough? Go buy a gun. You want to be powerful? You can't buy that; you must learn to be it.

I felt invincible. My strength was that of a giant. God was certainly standing beside me. I smashed five saloons with rocks before I ever took a hatchet.

Carry Nation

People have a
unique capacity
for innovation.
How many cats
have dreamed
up a new way of
catching mice?

**Life is about
taking chances.
Nothing
worthwhile
is ever a
sure thing.**

Idealists are magnificent and terrifying in equal measure. With others, if you can't defeat them, you can often reach a compromise, but those who are armored in their beliefs are immune to everything.

Physical courage is not a monopoly of those with physical strength.

A safe life would be one of pointlessness and tedium. Take a chance on life.

The greatest courage is simply to be oneself.

I often say of George Washington
that he was one of the few in the
whole history of the world who was
not carried away by power.

Robert Frost

If you would be taken care of,
you must be prepared to do
the job yourself.

If one is forever cautious, can one remain a human being?

To be in charge of others you must first be able to govern yourself.
Alexander Solzhenitsyn

Integrity is better than armor.

Break what you have to do into bite-sized chunks. The seemingly impossible can often be attained if you do it bit by bit. Even climbing Mount Everest is only a series of single steps.

The best people have a core like a steel spring—it may bend but it never snaps.

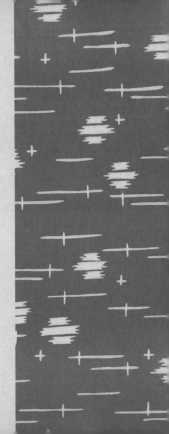

The best ruler is only a shadowy
presence to his subjects. Next comes
the one they love. Next the one they fear.
The worst is the one they treat lightly.

Tao Te Ching

**Work at your own pace and your
strength will never leave you.
Knowing the rhythms of your body
will make you ten times stronger.**

It is remarkable how people will carry
on in the face of insuperable difficulties
and overwhelming odds just because
giving up seems unthinkable.

Power without responsibility:
the prerogative of the harlot
through the ages.

Rudyard Kipling

It's no good saying, "I did my best."
Sometimes you just have to succeed.

**Governing a large state is
like boiling a small fish.**

Tao Te Ching

"I've lost everything except my trousers," said the earthquake victim. "What will you do now?" asked the reporter. "Oh, I'll survive," was the reply.

Humor is a peculiarly human form of power and it is particularly aggravating to the pompous.

The strength that wins is calm
and had an exhaustless source in
its passive depth.

Rabindranath Tagore

A capacity for telling the truth is a
huge source of strength. Liars may win
small advantages, but nothing can
compensate for the loss of reputation.

You are full of potential miracles. The risk is worth it.

You're going to die sooner or later, but that is not the point. The point is what are you going to do between now and then?

The burden is equal to the horse's strength.

Talmud

A friend, no longer in the first flush of youth, volunteered for a charity parachute jump. "How will you do it?" everyone asked her. "Easy, there's only one way down and you don't need a road map."

People desperate for power
are those least suited to use it.

**The power of humans lies in their
ability to endlessly resist the
ravages of other humans.**

If you can conquer others, you are strong,
but to conquer yourself takes wisdom.

The mastery of nature is vainly believed to be an adequate substitute for self mastery.

Reinhold Niebuhr

A mighty tree is uprooted by a great wind. The reed, although not so mighty, just bends as the wind goes by.

A person of true conviction must be prepared to act alone.

The strength of your convictions can be a source of great power, so examine those convictions closely.

Even governments only tax people according to their means.

We can all think of something that is the worst that can happen to us yet, when it at last happens, we find we can cope.

In eastern martial arts you practice one movement again and again and again until it becomes second nature. The point of this is that when you need it, you don't have to waste time thinking about it.

Tackling problems head-on is stupid. Learn from judo players and choose the time and manner of your attack carefully.

An acquaintance was going to donate a kidney to his son who needed a transplant. Everyone told him how brave he was. "No," he replied, "if it was your son you'd do just the same."

A strong body is good, but
a strong mind is invaluable.

**When it is a question of "do or die"
who will choose to die?**

Train hard, fight easy.
Marshal Suvarov

**When it comes to the pinch
human beings are heroic.**

George Orwell

Knowing
exactly who
you are and
what you
are good for
is like having
an army on
your side.

There are very few monsters that merit the fears we have of them.

André Gide

Keep your nose clean. In life there are always those who look for your weaknesses but, if you have none, they will be greatly discouraged.

Sincerity is a terrible weapon. People are used to others being insincere and when they discover someone who isn't, they are greatly unsettled.

Nine times out of ten the best thing that can happen to a young man is to be tossed overboard and compelled to sink or swim.

James A. Garfield

It's no good lying around being afraid. Get out there and act, then you won't be afraid any more.

Courage mounteth with occasion.

Shakespeare

Your fears are enemy spies that secretly undermine your defenses. Like all spies, they should be taken out and shot.

Hitler wrote about what he was going to do and no one believed him. Openness and sincerity are excellent qualities in good hands, but quite terrifying in bad ones.

The remarkable thing about the Holocaust was not that so many people died, but the sheer tenacity that enabled the others to survive.

The human spirit can be stamped on repeatedly and beaten flat, but like some sort of rubber ball, it always springs right back into shape when the pressure is removed.

If you need to lean on someone,
make sure it's the one in the mirror.

What one has to do
usually can be done.
Eleanor Roosevelt

Taking risks is a form of security.
Whenever you are at risk, you
summon up reserves of grit,
ingenuity, and tenacity that help to
compensate for the extra danger.

If you want safety, you'll never leave home, and even then you won't be safe.

God, who gave burdens, also gave shoulders.

Yiddish proverb

In ancient Japan, an official was once offered a bribe. "Go on, take it," said his tempter, "no one will know." "You know, I know, heaven knows, and earth knows," was the reply.

Being right in an unpopular cause is one of the toughest tests of our strength.

Think for yourself. Everybody tells you to do this from the moment you start school but nobody ever really means it. If you doubt me, try doing it at a university.

The majority are not always right. Hitler was elected by a majority.

The strong person is not the one who can deal with the occasional crisis, but the one who can persevere through all difficulties day by day.

The world has seen enough of tyrants now to know one thing for sure—they ain't so tough.

Better to take a chance now than live perpetually in fear.

Danger and delight grow on one stalk.

English proverb

You don't get
the fruit without
climbing the tree.

Those who cling to life die and
those who defy death live.

Uyesugi Kenshin

No one gets to be a hero by playing safe.

You need to dare and dare and dare. It stops you getting bored.

What sets the superior person apart is the ability to produce new ideas and to introduce vibrant new colors to the human palette.

Take physical risks and you'll be admired, but the real challenge is to think dangerously.

So long as you think "difficulty" and "danger" your thinking is blocked by these concepts. Throw them out and the blockage will disappear.

The best way out of a problem is through it.

Proverb

Courage is not a man with a gun. Any dope knows how to fire a gun.

You can't catch salmon standing on the bank.

Facing your own faults and doing something about them takes more guts than many are willing to admit.

If you would
be strong,
root out
your faults.

It takes
courage to
stand up and
speak, but
also to sit
down and
listen.

Accepting a new idea can be as challenging as jumping off a cliff.

It's easy to think in black and white, but life is subtle and, to understand it, you need to see the shades of gray.

The real test of courage comes when everyone tells you that you're wrong.

Strong people can afford to be gentle. Only the weak and insecure need to throw their weight around.

A strong body is excellent, but a strong mind is best.

A bold heart is half the battle.

No one should be in charge of your life but you. Anyone else is a dictator that you need to overthrow.

Strength, like character, is best built slowly but surely.

Have the strength to think new thoughts. Common sense is common enough, but rarely sensible.

Nothing can resist an idea whose time has come.

Generals can win by force of arms, but Gandhi defied an empire using nothing but peaceful resistance.

Always think the unthinkable. You don't have to do what you're thinking, but you should know what it feels like to think freely.

A strong person may not look strong until the chips are down. There's no point flexing your muscles just for the heck of it.

Why does "we're all grown-ups here" always imply "and we're about to do something we should be ashamed of"?

Still waters run deep.

"Sorry" is only the hardest
word for people of poor spirit.

**Always have the strength
to admit you were wrong.**

Whatever you do, presume that other people know. They probably do.

Everyone who can do what is necessary for his or her family and friends on a daily basis is a hero.

What the world calls a "strong man" is sometimes a weak man with bullies for friends.

Who was the stronger character, Stalin or Mandela?

Strength persuades opponents to become friends.

Why is
one of the
world's
greatest
symbols
of strength
a man
nailed to
a cross?

Published by MQ Publications Limited
12 The Ivories, 6–8 Northampton Street
London N1 2HY
Tel: 020 7359 2244   Fax: 020 7359 1616
email: mail@mqpublications.com

Text © Robert Allen 2003
Design: Philippa Jarvis

ISBN: 1-84072-560-5

3 5 7 9 0 8 6 4 2

Printed and bound in China